1

WASHINGTON STATE

A PICTURE BOOK TO REMEMBER HER BY

Designed by
DAVID GIBBON

Produced by
TED SMART

Photography by
Edmund Nägele F.R.P.S.

CRESCENT BOOKS
NEW YORK

INTRODUCTION

In the northwest corner of the U.S.A. lies the state of Washington. To the north is the Canadian province of British Columbia, to the east and south the states of Idaho and Oregon respectively, and to the west the Pacific Ocean.

Washington became the 42nd member of the United States in 1889 but it has a far longer recorded history, much of it related to the many attempts that were made to find the elusive Northwest Passage, the sea route from the Atlantic, round the north of Canada to the Pacific. In 1497, King Henry VII of England sent John Cabot, and later many other famous explorers tried their luck: Jacques Cartier, Sir Francis Drake, Sir Martin Frobisher, Captain James Cook and Henry Hudson.

Other early visitors to the area were Catholic and Protestant missionaries, who attempted to convert the Indians living there; men like Marcus Whitman and the Reverend Henry Spalding. They believed that it was essential for the Indians to come under the influence of the white man and so, when the Oregon Trail opened, they encouraged white settlers to travel to the Pacific Northwest. The first thousand reached the area in 1843. On the whole relations between white men and Indians were friendly, but on occasions treaties were broken and the result was often armed conflict.

Whitman and Spalding built houses, churches and schools, and Whitman built a mission among the Cayuse Indians, near present-day Walla Walla. He tried to teach the Cayuse to till the earth, irrigate and grind corn, but they were disinterested in his ideas. The 'Whitman Massacre' took place after an epidemic of measles broke out. Although they were given the same treatment and care as the white children, many of the less resistant Indian children died. Suspecting sorcery, the Indians killed 14 whites and kidnapped 53 women and children. This led to the Cayuse War.

The enormous fur trade that developed in the Pacific Northwest was probably triggered off by one of Captain James Cook's voyages in 1778, when he secured sea-otter skins from the Indians and sold them, very profitably, in the Orient. Trappers flocked to the Pacific Northwest, lured by large numbers of mink, weasel, ermine, lynx, fox, beaver, muskrat and racoon, to mention just a few of the fur-bearing animals that thrived there. The British Hudson Bay Company swiftly moved in and organised the trade in most of the territory. By 1812 the United States dominated the fur trade in the region, although the Hudson's Bay Company retained several strongholds until the 1840s.

This part of America was known as Oregon Country but in 1848 Congress established the Oregon Territory which included all of Oregon, Washington and Idaho, as well as parts of Montana and Wyoming. It was an enormous area; sparsely populated and with poor communications, it proved virtually impossible to govern. Public demand forced Congress to create Washington Territory in 1853, but it was to be many years before Washington acquired its present-day boundaries.

Seattle is Washington's chief city and the largest metropolis of the Pacific Northwest. Its site, between the Puget Sound and Lake Washington, has enabled it to become an important Pacific port, and the gateway to both Alaska and the Orient. The first settlement was at Alki Point in 1851, and two years later a town was laid out, named after the Suquamish Indian Chief Seatlh. Its early function was as a saw milling centre and its early history eventful. In 1856 it was the focus of an Indian attack; in the 1880s it survived anti-Chinese riots and in 1889 it suffered a devastating fire. Like the rest of the state, development was slow until the Great Northern Railway arrived in 1893, when Seattle became a major rail terminus. Its growth was boosted again during the gold rush era in the Yukon and Alaska, when the harbour became the main supply depot. Other events which were to prove a stimulus to Seattle's growth were the opening of the Panama Canal in 1914, the construction of the Lake Washington Ship Canal and the building of fifty miles of wharves, which turned the city into an international seaport. During World War II the shipyards were at full capacity and the aircraft industry boomed. Today, important industries include aerospace, forest products, food processing, insurance and electronics. The city has a large fishing fleet and in 1962 it hosted the World Fair.

At the falls of the Spokane River is the city of Spokane, the centre of a lumbering and mining region. It was frequented by trappers when the North West Company established a trading post there in 1810. Settled in 1871, it was incorporated ten years later when the Northern Pacific Railway arrived. Like Seattle, it was almost destroyed by a fire in 1889 and had to be extensively rebuilt.

Tacoma is situated on Commencement Bay, Puget Sound, in West Washington and it grew up as a port and saw-milling centre. Today, it has shipyards, smelters, foundries, electrochemical plants and food processing factories.

The state capital, Olympia, is at the southern end of the Puget Sound, at the mouth of the Deschutes River. It was laid out in 1851 as Smithfield, and became the site of a U.S. Customs house. It was renamed Olympia after the Olympic Mountains nearby, and became the state capital in 1853. It boasts two Capitol Buildings, one dating back to 1893, the other to 1935.

Washington's terrain is dominated by the high Cascade Range, which runs parallel to the coast and divides the land into a western one third and an eastern two thirds. The former experiences some of the highest rainfalls in America and has densely-wooded rain forests extending along the western slopes. The eastern two thirds is a rain shadow area producing large tracts of desert but, with the aid of comprehensive irrigation schemes, arable and livestock rearing farms flourish.

The Cascades Range contains a number of spectacular peaks of volcanic origin, the highest being 14,410 foot Mount Rainier. The mountains are a favourite retreat for tourists as well as helping to supply hydroelectric power, irrigation and industry. Forestry is important and much of the 23 million acres of forest in this attractive state is still virgin timber.

The famous "Hall of Mosses", in Olympic National Park's magnificent Rain Forest on the upper Hoh River, can be seen *left*.

Spokane, established as the early trading post of the Pacific Northwest, is today the second largest city in Washington State. One of the city's favourite attractions, Riverfront Park *these pages*, located along the Spokane River and built on the former site of the 1974 World Exposition, contains a wealth of features including the hand-carved antique Carousel *top left*, the IMAX Theater, Opera House and Convention Center, as well as the appealing Childrens' Zoo and ever-popular funfair with its thrilling rides.

Dedicated in 1974, Spokane's tranquil Nishinomiya Garden *this page*, with its vermilion Ceremonial Bridge *above*, reveals the exquisite art of a Japanese garden where delightful waterfalls and still pools, carefully-placed stones and ornamental stone lanterns blend to perfection amid exotic vegetation.

From the Spokane Falls Gondola Ride can be seen a spectacular view of the mighty Spokane Falls *left*.

Still retaining its early, pioneering spirit, Spokane, the county seat since 1879, seen in the aerial views *above right and centre left,* was originally founded as a trading post by the Northwest Fur Company, in 1810, some ten miles from its present position, alongside Little Spokane River. Settled in 1871, when the nucleus of today's city was established at Spokane Falls, the site was formally laid out seven years later, and incorporated in 1881 when the Northern Pacific Railway reached the city. With abundant waterpower and a rich hinterland yielding agriculture, forests and minerals, the city prospered, becoming the largest railroad centre west of Omaha, as well as the economic and cultural centre for a four-state area known as the "Inland Empire". In 1889, a disastrous fire razed much of the city, but with great determination and the resultant burst of rebuilding, the city was reincorporated under its present name, in 1900. With developments in metal, lumber and food-processing industries, and the expansion of the nearby Coeur d'Alene mineral field, producing gold, silver, copper and uranium, as well as the completion of the Grand Coulee Dam Project in 1941, its industrial and financial success was assured.

Howard Street *top left* and Main Street with Lincoln Square *below right* are situated in the downtown area *bottom left,* where a unique system of inter-connected skybridges provide excellent 'mall-type' shopping, whilst *below* can be seen the lofty steeple of Spokane's magnificent St John's Cathedral.

Heavy-eared corn ready for harvesting *left*, and rolling waves of unripened grain seen from Steptoe Butte *previous page,* are part of the rich farmland of the Palouse, which ranks amongst the most productive in the world. Backed by rugged mountains, the Snake River is shown at Lyon's Ferry *above, centre right and below right,* and south of Clarkston *below* as the Idaho Queen leaves a trail of silver spume across the river's surface. *Top right* can be seen the Palouse Falls and *overleaf* the Palouse River as it winds through craggy canyons and sage-brush hills to join the Snake River.

Providing hydroelectric power and navigation, McNary Lock and Dam is the easternmost of four multipurpose dams on the Columbia River. *Left and below* can be seen the navigation lock and spillway; *top right* the lock and north shore fish ladder which affords a passageway for steelhead trout and species of Pacific salmon, and *centre right* the fish viewing room.

Overlooking the Columbia River, Stonehenge *bottom right* is a replica of the famous site on Salisbury Plain, England. Pictured *overleaf* is majestic Mt. Adams mirrored in the still waters of Takhlakh Lake, whilst *above* a giant sunflower greets the visitor to this, the "Evergreen State".

Snow-tipped mountains and sparkling waterfalls, forests of conifer and pine, and rugged coastlines reveal Washington's appeal, in this land of striking contrast. In the Gifford Pinchot National Forest a veiled waterfall cascades by Spirit Lake *below left* as snow-capped Mt. St Helens, seen *above* with Yale Lake, rises beyond the Spirit Lake shore *left*.

Fort Vancouver National Historic Site is shown *above and centre right* and picturesque Ilwaco Harbour *top right*, whilst perched on their rocky promontories overlooking the Columbia River mouth are the lighthouses, at North Head *below,* and at Cape Disappointment *bottom right,* which is seen shrouded in mist *overleaf.*

Mounds of oyster-shells are shown *centre left* at South Bend, the 'Oyster Capital of the World', in the lovely Willapa Bay area, with its tranquil harbours such as those at Willapa *top left* and Tokeland *bottom left*, whilst to the north of the Bay, the silver waves of the Pacific lap popular Grayland Beach *right*.

OYSTERS
SOLD HERE

Bleached trees line the sandy coastline at Queets *right* in the spectacular Olympic National Park where an uninvited guest joins picnickers in one of the park's recreation areas *above*. *Overleaf* is shown a further view of the Hall of Mosses in the dense rain forest, and *top and bottom* the State Legislative Building which dominates the skyline of Olympia, the State Capital.

Between glacier-clad mountains and unspoiled ocean shores, evidenced in Rialto Beach *left and bottom right*, the scenic wilderness of Olympic National Park embraces majestic lakes, such as beautiful Crescent Lake *centre right*, and dense, coniferous rain forests *below*. Formed from the earth's crust by the relentless squeezing along a contact zone between two giant crustal plates, the sculptured peaks of the Olympic Range tower beyond the thickly forested conifers *above*. Spectacular sunsets over Great Bend on Hood Canal, flanking the Park's eastern border, are shown *top right and overleaf*.

Turrets, wrought iron work and
'gingerbread' decorations ornament the
fascinating Victorian houses *above and
facing page,* in Port Townsend, one of the
state's oldest cities, overlooking Puget
Sound.

Anchored at Bremerton, the U.S.S.
Missouri *below* was the site of the historic
signing of the United States' treaty with
Japan in 1945, whilst *right* can be seen the
picturesque marina at Poulsbo, a delightful
Scandinavian community.

Heavily laden stalls piled high with a colourful array of unusual vegetables and fruits, seafoods and meats, are a particular feature of Pike Place *these pages*, Seattle's rambling public market-place which was originally established in 1907. With its additional flea market, arts and crafts fair and facing sophisticated shops, the all-weather market is a popular place to shop.

Soaring skyscrapers in downtown Seattle can be seen in the superb view *overleaf*.

Rising over 600 feet above the Seattle Center, the lofty Space Needle *above left* provides panoramic views from its observation deck which is reached by a high-speed toll elevator *centre right.* This impressive landmark can be seen *top,* reflected in the shimmering façade of the Safeco Building; through the "Changing Form" on Queen Anne Hill *left,* and from the Pacific Science Center *below and bottom right. Above* is shown the Monorail and Washington Plaza Hotel, and *top right* the Ranier Bank Tower.

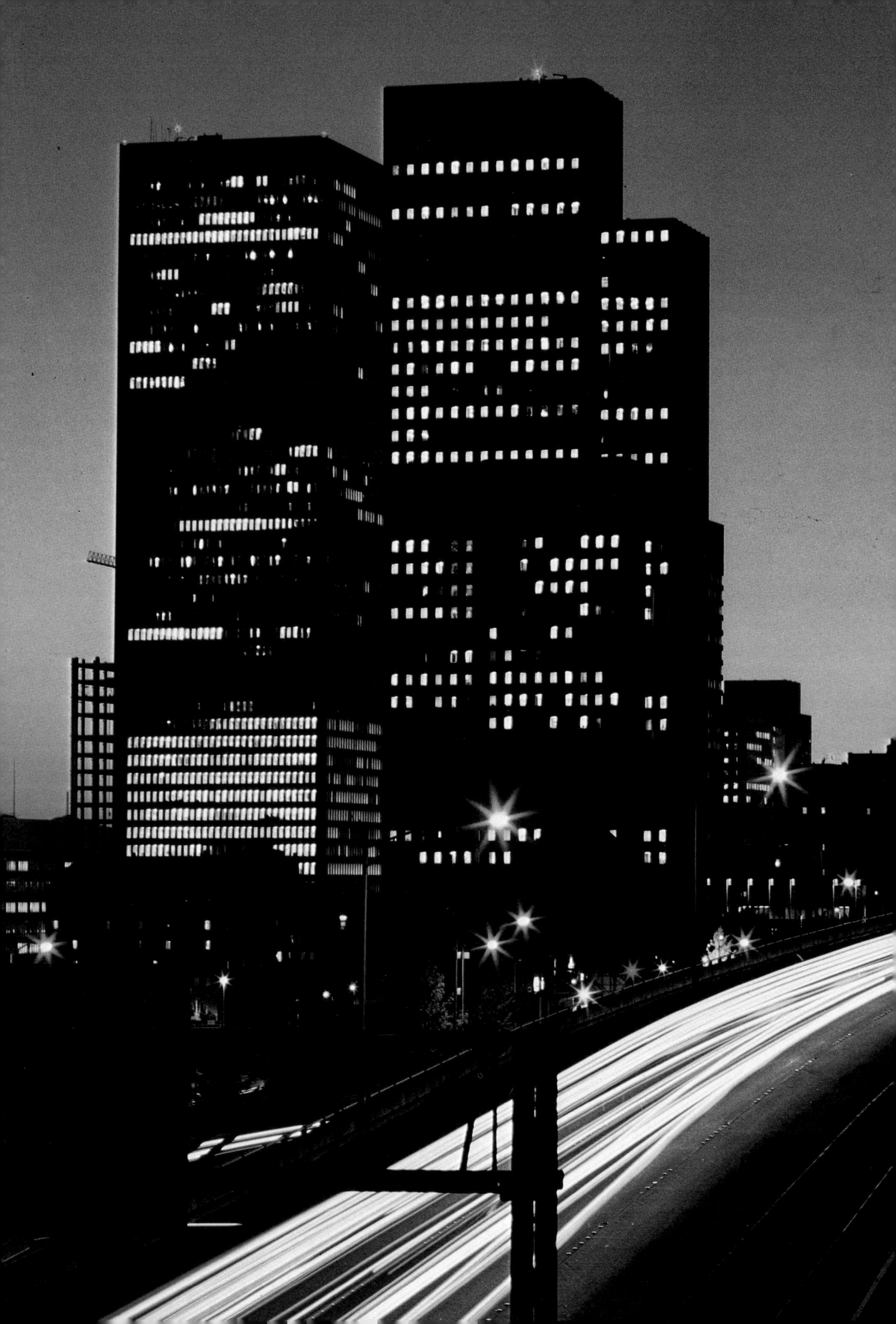

Seattle's exciting skyline, fanning outwards towards the horizon, where snow-capped Mt. Rainier appears to float in a misty sea *bottom right,* is seen from the Space Needle *above.* Against a backdrop of twinkling lights, the downtown area and illuminated Space Needle is shown *left* from Queen Anne Hill, whilst Interstate Highway 5 curves past the starkly outlined skyscrapers *previous page. Centre right* can be seen Waterfront Park, and *below and top right* the Monorail track that leads to the circular column of the Washington Plaza Hotel.

Seattle, the "Queen City", with its "great outdoor" atmosphere, boasts a wealth of recreational facilities that cater for every taste. Illustrated *on these pages* are scenes around this colourful city which include the fun and excitement of the Fun Forest in Elliott Park *facing page,* and the Seattle Fair, with its torchlight procession *bottom left. Above* can be seen one of the Fire Department's powerful fire-boats which are moored at historic Fire Station No. 5, established in 1889, after the great Fire, and *below* the International Fountain in the Seattle Center.

In splendid isolation the snow-encrusted peaks of majestic Mt. Rainier *above* rise to a height of 14, 410 feet in the superb Mt. Rainier National Park. Encircled by a forest of conifers, the mountain peaks can be seen *previous page*, near Paradise; *below* from Ricksecker Point, and *bottom left* beyond Tipsoo Lake and Yakima Peak which towers above the flower-carpeted valley floor *top left. Centre left* is pictured the Grove of the Patriarchs, and *right* jewel-like Bench Lake.

During the summer months, when wildflowers follow the melting snow, the undulating, subalpine meadowland at Paradise *below* is filled with a profusion of beautiful blossoms, such as the avalanche lilies *bottom right* and silky blue lupines *right*, which provide a riot of colour between the shady, forested groves.

Falls Creek *left*, Narada Falls *top* and Christine Falls *below* are among the many sparkling waterfalls that cascade over creviced rocks in Mt. Rainier National Park.

"Welcome to Leavenworth", proclaims the sign *below* – to this enchanting Bavarian village *left,* with its gaily decorated plaques *above* and timbered and stucco buildings adorned with elaborate paintings and flower-bedecked balconies. Nestled amid Washington's forest-covered mountain slopes, the village is a popular year-round recreation centre.

The Grand Coulee, seen from Crown Point Vista with Franklin D. Roosevelt Lake *bottom left,* is one of the largest concrete dams in the world, harnessing the Columbia River for irrigation, power and flood control. Among the many visitor attractions at this vast hydroelectric complex, are the fascinating murals *left and below,* in the Power Generating Plant. Situated at the head of the Lower Grand Coulee, Dry Falls, considered to be one of the world's geological wonders, is shown *above right,* and *right,* 25-Mile Creek on Lake Chelan, which is seen in the superb aerial view with Chelan *overleaf.*

In Lake Chelan's scenic vicinity *above*, apple orchards dot the lake's deep blue shores in the outstanding aerial view *left*, and along the Columbia River *top left.* The famous Red and Golden delicious apples, noted for their superior colour and flavour, thrive in the area's clear, dry, sunny climate.

In the popular tourist attraction of Winthrop, originally founded by Guy Waring in the late 19th century, rows of false-fronted buildings, wooden sidewalks and old-fashioned street lighting *top, right and below,* are reminiscent of the town's colourful 'boom mining' days.

Separating the moist coastal region from the arid interior, the majestic Cascade Range, with its jagged, snowy crests *left and bottom right*, is marked by its extinct volcanic peaks, glaciated lakes and dense stands of towering firs. Mt. Shuksan *top right* is shown *previous page* rising beyond the rippled waters of Picture Lake; *above* can be seen Diablo Lake and Mt. Challenger; *centre right* Liberty Bell Mt. and Early Winter Spires at Washington Pass on the North Cascades Highway; *below* a dramatic sunset over Fish Lake, and *overleaf* remote Glacier Peak, visible in the background of the Cascades' snow-filled canyons.

Pictured on page 64 is the historical Border House, near Silverlake.

Text filmsetting by Acesetters Ltd., Richmond, Surrey, England.
Printed and bound in Barcelona, Spain by Cronion, S.A.
1987 edition published by Crescent Books, distributed by Crown Publishers, Inc.
ISBN 0 517 28866 4
hgfedcbcba

Dep. Leg. B-40279-87